Praise for *Jacob the Baker*
and his heartwarming adventures

"Jacob will show you things that you may have known once, but probably forgot in the modern hustle and bustle of life today."

—*Jewish Post & Opinion*

"benShea is a serious philosopher who believes the world is hungry for a wise and simpler kindness."

—*The Portland Oregonian*

"Jacob's journey is our journey. With him we ascend past fear and arrive at wisdom."

—Eugene Schwartz
Philanthropist

"Jacob serves as a powerful reminder that there is greatness in simplicity, and there must be simplicity in greatness. He has definitely left his mark on my life."

—Rabbi Simcha Weinberg
Lincoln Square Synagogue, New York City

"Once again with *Jacob's Ladder*, Noah benShea has elevated the human spirit to great heights with wisdom."

—Howard Schultz
Chairman and CEO of STARBUCKS

Also by Noah benShea

Jacob the Baker

Jacob's Journey

Great Jewish Quotes

The Word

Jacob's Ladder

Jacob's Ladder

Wisdom for the Heart's Ascent

Noah benShea

Ballantine Books • New York

A Ballantine Book
Published by The Ballantine Publishing Group

http://www.randomhouse.com

Library of Congress Catalog Card Number: 98-96016

ISBN: 0-345-40438-6

Cover design by Cathy Colbert
Cover illustration by David Frampton

This edition published by arrangement with Villard Books, a registered trademark of Random House, Inc.

Manufactured in the United States of America

First Ballantine Books Edition: July 1998

10 9 8 7 6 5 4 3 2 1

For my mother,
who is caring
and wise
and of great courage,

&

For my father,
who is with me
always

*"My son, if your heart is wise,
my heart too will be glad."*

—*Proverbs 23:15*

Contents

Jacob's Ladder

Look Backward to See Forward

Once there was a baker named Jacob.

He was a poor but pious man who lived an anonymous life in a timeless village. While he waited in the early mornings for the ovens to come to temperature, he would write little notes to himself in an effort to make sense of his life.

Then, unknown to Jacob, one of his notes was accidentally baked into a loaf of bread. A woman who purchased the bread came upon the note and was incredibly moved by the wisdom and compassion of what she read.

Rushing to meet Jacob, this wise and gentle baker, she found a long ignored and unrecognized treasure.

Soon the secret of Jacob the Baker spread like a whisper that rode the wind. People—even from surrounding communities—stopped Jacob on his way to work; they waited for him at his home; they crowded the bakery where he worked. They *asked Jacob questions about prayer and friendship and charity and whatever was troubling their soul. Children appeared after school and sat on the flour sacks, listening to his stories.*

Before long, however, all this attention made it impossible for Jacob to remain in his own community. And so he packed his few belongings and embarked on a long journey—only to find that his reputation inevitably preceded him and that destiny is never at a distance.

Now Jacob has returned home.

He lives alone, a simple baker once again. The village has regained its balance. Time and respect have calmed the waters.

People, of course, still seek Jacob's wisdom. But a winter night is dissolving, and the morning star has just appeared . . .

We Are Alone Together

Jacob turned over and stared into the rough beams that formed the ribs of his ceiling. The moments before dawn threw a wash of light against the walls. Jacob took pause and wondered if he had woken in the belly of a great whale. He shut his eyes again and thanked God for the new day.

The cold in the small room, like icy fingers, urged him to his feet. Rising slowly, Jacob marveled at what a burden a man could be to himself.

At the center of his narrow table, a dark bread sat next to a small dish of salt. With two hands, Jacob lifted the bread in a blessing. Lowering the offering, Jacob gently rained salt from between his thumb and forefinger onto the crust and looked up. Then, pinching the heel of the loaf, he pulled the crust backward, breaking his fast.

The simplicity of Jacob's needs enriched his life. In wanting less he was afforded more.

Jacob put his arms into the cocoon of the heavy coat he would wear for the walk to the bakery. He opened the door and slipped out into the morning. Snow from the previous night covered the earth.

Like a single point of paint, he moved across a blank canvas. A wind blew behind him, erasing his steps as he walked.

A line of ice had formed around the frame of the bakery's back doors, making it necessary for Jacob to shoulder them open. When the ice cracked, it sounded like a small branch breaking underfoot. The pigeons at the base of the loading dock looked up from their labor of uncovering seeds and crumbs. He was warmed by their company and their ritual.

As he stepped into the bakery, the floor creaked under his weight; it was a familiar groan. The darkness enveloped him and Jacob accepted its embrace. It, too, was familiar.

Inspecting the shadows, Jacob paused. It is strange, he thought, where we take root. We are like seeds in the wind who wake in the darkness.

Jacob drew a single match from the bread bench beside the oven and bent to light the pilot flame. The blue teardrop leapt and danced along the row of burners. Be of service, thought Jacob. One may light many.

He stood slowly, stretched his back, and from his back pocket retrieved a pencil. Locating the scraps of paper he kept in small piles near the dough scales, he began to write.

Like the ancient shepherd, Jacob heard psalms in the wind.

When others told Jacob that what he wrote reflected great wisdom, Jacob answered, "My writing is wiser than I am."

When they said, "You are just being humble," Jacob answered, "God is always in concert. But the audience is not always listening."

Jacob began to roll out the dough that had been resting overnight. The heat from the warming ovens hung above him like a blanket suspended. Jacob curled into the comfort. He wondered if perhaps he was still in bed, dreaming.

Then, while his hands worked the dough, he thought about the homes in his village. He saw husbands and wives only now just awakening. He saw sons and daughters with eyes like giant almonds holding the hopeful years ahead of them. He saw his own home: the empty bed and the shallow grave of his own impression still in the sheets.

He hovered over himself, suddenly lonely. It was an unaccustomed feeling. He wondered how loneliness could creep up behind a man who had for so many years felt at peace with his solitary life.

"Halloo!" a voice behind him boomed, startling Jacob and breaking the full, still moment.

Max, a young baker, carrying a sack of flour toward the mixer, repented, "Sorry, Jacob, I didn't mean to surprise you. Are you alone?"

Jacob turned to Max. "We are alone together," said Jacob.

Soon the two men stood shoulder to shoulder, using the heels of their hands to shape the lines of loaves.

"Jacob, do you mind if I ask you a question?" asked Max.

Jacob didn't respond but lifted a pan filled with the unbaked breads and set it on a rack.

"Jacob," asked Max, surprised, "are you ignoring me?"

"I was just wondering if I have been ignoring myself," said Jacob. He made the statement almost absently, laying down the prospect of it like flour scattered onto the bread boards.

Max was puzzled. He had never previously witnessed Jacob confused in his feelings.

Sensing Max's discomfort, Jacob put a hand on his shoulder and said, "In life we often discover what we did not know we were seeking."

"I'll tell you what I'm looking for," interjected Samuel, the owner of the bakery, who had also arrived without warning. Samuel moved his wide form around the mixer, already talking as if he were midstream in the conversation. "I'm looking for the rest of my bakers *and* my customers."

Then, nodding and noting the morning's progress, he said, "Bless you, Jacob. You and you alone I can count on." A conductor lost in his own rhythm, Samuel waved his finger while he spoke.

"And what of Max?" asked Jacob, reminding Samuel of his manners.

"When Max is here as many years as you, I'll bless him too."

"Bless the moment, Samuel," said Jacob, "and the years will be their own blessing. Many of us live life in a rush because it allows us to believe we are going somewhere."

"You hear that, Max?" said Samuel as Max left to retrieve another sack of flour. "Even when I say nothing, this man turns it into something."

"I'm a baker," said Jacob, sidestepping the compliment. "From flour I make bread. But the grain that makes the flour is a gift from God."

Samuel laughed and patted the outline of his stomach under his smock. "And what a gift it is, eh?"

"Your friendship has been a great gift to me," said Jacob.

"And I appreciate your wisdom," said Samuel, again wagging his finger, "even if I don't always know what you are feeling."

"Sometimes our heart holds secrets even from ourselves," said Jacob quietly.

Other voices entered the bakery, fracturing the shell surrounding the three men. The balance of the bakers arrived like knots connected one to another by their greetings and what was soon the interlocking of their efforts.

Pans and carts were rolled to the ovens with promise and pulled away with treasure stacks of golden loaves. Cookies, like so many coins, fell from trays into racks and were hurried, soft and hot, to the front.

There, hands from the village dropped their coins and hurried home warmed by the breads they carried under their coats.

In this throb of activity, the moments moved under Jacob like a river; another day in the bakery drifted, unaware, true to itself.

And then the day was done. Dawn had spun to dusk.

Dressing for a Transformation

Preparing for the journey home, Jacob once again wrapped himself in his heavy coat, not knowing that he was dressing for a transformation.

A river, which threaded the community, stitched the inhabitants together in a common fabric. Jacob followed it home. Thick soups with their bubbling broth steamed the windows in some of the houses that Jacob passed. He remembered once standing in a kitchen next to his mother and marking his name on a foggy pane of glass. He remembered his father. He remembered the loss. And then he stopped remembering.

When Jacob raised his eyes from the path and saw a small figure sitting at his doorstep, he felt his heart stirred by the thought of company. "Thank you," mouthed Jacob inaudibly, knowing to Whom he expressed appreciation.

Advancing closer, he saw a very young man. The boy, in anticipation, stood up and tried to brush the caked-on dirt from his trousers.

Waving an open hand toward the boy, Jacob motioned him to stop: "If you take the journey from your clothes," said Jacob, sensing the youth's unease, "I will be forced to dust the flour from my own clothes."

"Then you are Jacob the Baker," stated the boy with resolve.

"I am trying to be," said Jacob.

The answer was not what the boy expected. And yet he now raced ahead: "How did you know I have been on a journey?"

"Have you ever thought you were not?" answered Jacob in a tone both considerate and clever.

The boy contemplated Jacob's response without answering.

Jacob smiled. "Good. Silence is the wisest first answer to any question."

"If a question's first answer is silence, what is the second?"

"Compassion," said Jacob. "Come inside where it is warm."

"But you don't know me or my name," protested the boy. "Why are you inviting me into your home?"

"Okay," said Jacob. "I'm cold. Who are you?"

Now the boy laughed. "I'm cold too."

"My point exactly," said Jacob, and he motioned to the boy to enter the small home.

But the boy stood his ground, shaking his head. "I am not allowed to enter your home until you have read this," and he handed Jacob a neatly addressed note.

Jacob accepted the sealed letter slowly and began to read while eyeing the youth over the top of the page. The two stood together in the dying light.

Dear Jacob,

Many years have passed since the stories of Jacob the Baker reached the Council of Sages. At first there were tales of your wisdom, and I was not curious. But then word of your humility and compassion, and the reality of my own ill health, made our meeting inevitable.

When I appeared at the bakery in the guise of a pauper, you opened your heart and my mind. Later, when I revealed my true nature, you remained the same.

My years have been long, but every man's days are few. I had asked you to take my place as the Elder for the Council of Sages, but you chose to continue as a baker, and I am wiser for accepting this.

Soon I will be gone, and the communities will have no Elder for the Council. But I have a grandson who is young, and I have great hope for him. His name is Jonah. I ask you to take him into your heart. I ask you to be his teacher and lend him a father's shoulder; life has taken both his parents from him. I ask this as the last wish of a dying man.

Our scriptures say that it is not good for a man to live alone, and now Jonah is alone. As you are too. May he be a source of strength to you, as you have been to so many.

You are in my prayers. I await the pleasure of your company.

Yours in peace,
Ezra

The sky was turning black. Light from candles and fires in the village homes formed a pulsing circle around the boy and Jacob. Together they stood alone under heaven.

Jacob turned his head toward the stars and put his hand on Jonah's shoulder.

Dreams in the Lost and Found

It was Jonah's first night in Jacob's home. The boy sat on the edge of a chair, perched between exhaustion and sleep. Jacob was not sure how to proceed.

"Perhaps it is time for bed?"

"You're not my father," said Jonah.

Jacob didn't answer but let the suggestion of sleep rest and prepared for bed himself.

As he lay down, Jacob could see Jonah's determination wavering slightly. Jacob shut his eyes and prayed for direction.

He was woken several hours later by the boy's sobs. Jonah had fallen asleep in the chair and was now crying in his sleep.

Jacob went over and covered Jonah with a blanket.

The boy woke. He wiped his eyes in embarrassment. "I'm sorry I cried."

"God gave us tears so we could water our feelings and grow as people," said Jacob.

"I just have these bad dreams," said the boy, and then confessed, "I miss my parents."

"All of us have bad dreams," said Jacob. "Sometimes we dream about what we have lost, and sometimes about what we have not yet found."

We Grow Stronger
from Wrestling with Our Fears

"Jacob," asked Jonah as he fumbled in the dark preparing for bed, "are you strong?"

"Would you like me to be strong?" asked Jacob.

"Yes," said the boy. "Then I would know that bad things couldn't happen."

"No one is that strong," said Jacob, "but all of us grow stronger from wrestling with our fears."

We Know More Than We Think

Jonah slept in the simple bed Jacob had laid out in the alcove by the window. In the course of the night Jonah had pulled the flannel and then the wool blankets to the hollow at the nape of his neck. A small crust of bread the boy had been eating, before slumber overcame him, remained grasped in his folded hand.

Jacob, who sat in a chair across the room from the boy, had neither experience nor expectation with parenting. As he said his morning prayers, the quiet chorus of Jonah's exhalation was an unfamiliar echo.

Patience, thought Jacob. God is not done with me yet.

Jonah stirred. His eyes opened and found Jacob's. Neither of them dropped pebbles into the pond of their stare. They shared the calm. The morning dawned and caught its own reflection in the quiet waters. Somewhere a bird sent its voice across the distance.

Jonah wordlessly rose and filled the kettle for tea. The seeming familiarity in Jonah's effort had the air of someone who was waking in a world he had always known and whose absence had only been a visit elsewhere.

All straight lines become curves across time, thought Jacob. Every journey eventually becomes a journey home.

"I would like you to come to the bakery with me," said Jacob.

"What would I do there?" asked Jonah.

"Ask questions."

"And . . . ?"

"And pay attention."

"That's all?"

"More always begins as less."

For Jacob now, the familiar path to work was altogether new.

What Isn't Said Is Also Heard

The single sound accompanying Jacob and Jonah's journey to the bakery was the snow crunching beneath their boots.

"Jacob," asked Jonah, "do you mind if I ask you a question?"

"That was our agreement," said Jacob.

"Are your parents still alive?" The question was more thrown out than asked.

"In here," said Jacob, touching his heart.

"When did they die?"

"Long ago."

"What about your parents?" asked Jacob. "When did they pass away?"

"Last winter," said Jonah, refusing to meet Jacob's stare. "A terrible sickness came over our village. I almost died as well. Sometimes I wish I had."

"Why?" asked Jacob.

"Then I wouldn't be alone," said the boy.

"But you are no longer alone," said Jacob.

"No, I guess not," said Jonah, but his voice lacked conviction.

"Sometimes the people we love are gone," said Jacob, shutting his eyes, "but all of them are with us."

We Are Born Learning and Die Fools

Outside the back door to the bakery, Jacob stopped.

"This is where I met your grandfather for the first time," said Jacob, pointing to the steps below the loading dock.

"He often told me the story," said Jonah, his voice at the border of memory and vulnerability.

"Yes, but did he tell you of the pigeons?" asked Jacob. Before Jonah could answer, Jacob drew crumbs of bread from his pocket and sprinkled them on the boy's shoulders.

Sparrows and pigeons lifted from the bakery's roof and encircled Jonah. For moments they fluttered above his shoulders, snatching the crumbs as they cleaned his coat.

"I can feel the breeze from their wings on my face!" he marveled, watching the birds return to the roof's shingles.

"Perhaps they are angels appointed to keep an eye on you."

"And are you an angel, Jacob?"

"I don't know," said Jacob, stopping. "Maybe *you're* an angel who is here to keep an eye on me."

The boy beamed at the thought.

"What I do know," said Jacob, "is that to see angels, we must look with our heart. Be loving and others will see the angel in you." He then turned to unlock the back door.

Jonah caught Jacob's sleeve, causing him to turn. "Jacob," he said, "I promise I will try not to feel sad."

"Only do not feel sad about being sad," said Jacob. "Sadness and joy," continued Jacob, "are waves in our sea. Watch them rise and fall in your life."

Jonah stared at Jacob without blinking. "Jacob, do you ever feel sad?"

"Over time," said Jacob, "every wave washes ashore."

Nothing Is As Old As a New Idea

Jonah moved behind Jacob through the bakery. The boy was interested in everything, and his actions followed his curiosity. Jacob repeatedly found himself reminding the boy where to be cautious, what not to touch, what was too hot.

"Jacob, you're treating me like a baby," said Jonah.

"Instead of the grown man you are?" asked Jacob playfully.

"I'm older than you think," said the boy, holding a pose to make himself look taller.

"I see," said Jacob flatly.

Jacob returned to his efforts in the bakery, and Jonah joined him. When they had placed the last tray of loaves on the oven's carousel of racks, Jonah said, "My grandfather used to say, 'All work is sacred.' "

"Yes," said Jacob, "and we all have different jobs."

"And what is this young man's job in my bakery?" asked Samuel, indicating the boy and announcing his own presence.

"He can have mine," grunted Max, moving through the doorway, carrying a load of pans.

"Jonah," said Jacob, "is the grandson of Ezra, the Elder of the Council of Sages, may he rest in peace." Jacob waited a beat for the implication of his remark to set in.

"Ohhh," said Samuel, confused.

"And I've invited him to live and work with me," said Jacob.

"Ohhh," said Samuel, looking back and forth between Jacob and Jonah, still confused.

"The man with his mouth open," said Max, pointing to Samuel, "is Samuel. He owns the bakery, and . . ." Max yanked at Samuel's shirt, pulling him forward, "he was a great admirer of your grandfather's. I'm Max."

"And what about school?" Samuel asked Jonah tentatively.

"I will learn from Jacob!" said Jonah.

"And I will learn from you," said Jacob, finishing the thought.

Looking at his old friend, Samuel said coyly, "You are liable to learn more than you intended."

"Learning is a path, not a destination," said Jacob.

"Well, then," Samuel directed Max, "back to work!"

"You two are wise," said Max, pointing to Jacob and Jonah. "But him," he said, now nodding at Samuel, "him I understand."

It Is Only a Fool Who Thinks
He Is Too Wise to Work

While Jacob worked, a middle-aged man came into the bakery and without explanation moved between Jacob and Jonah.

"Jacob, I have a chance to make some money, but I need a little luck."

"A wise man once said, 'The harder I work, the luckier I get.'"

"And what do you get for all that hard work?"

Jacob began pulling pans of bread from the oven. He mopped his brow with the back of his sleeve. "The sages say there is no greater reward than the rest of a working man."

"Listen," said the man. "Only fools work."

"No," said Jacob, "it is only a fool who thinks he is too wise to work."

When We Look at Others
We See Ourselves

A number of the children in the community came after school to see Jacob. They sat on the flour sacks, giggling and laughing, waiting for him to pause from his work. One of them pointed at Jonah and whispered to the others. Jonah noticed the children but stayed close to Jacob. When Jacob moved over toward the gathering, Jonah held to the periphery, watching.

"Jacob," said one of the girls coyly, "do you have a new helper?"

"This is Jonah," said Jacob. Jonah held his silence and stared at the floor. "And we all need help," added Jacob.

"Is that because you're getting older, Jacob?" asked one of the boys.

"Asking for help," said Jacob, "doesn't mean you are old, and it might mean you are wise."

"Old people can't do anything by themselves," said another boy.

"What can you do by yourself?" asked Jacob.

"I'm young and strong," boasted the boy. "I can do anything."

"But without others," said Jacob, "who could you brag to about this strength?"

"So when we look at others we see ourselves," said a little girl.

"Yes," said Jacob, "and sometimes the only thing less flattering than a bad mirror is a good one."

Be Who You Will Have
Your Children Become

Jonah stood behind Jacob as he locked the bakery for the evening. "Jacob," said the boy with purpose, "I'd like to talk with you about something."

They began down the path by the river. Above them, like incandescent patterns on the sky's black dome, the bright outlines of warriors and bears were framed in the geometry of the stars.

"Jacob," said Jonah, exhaling, "do you ever think about your mother?"

"Yes," said Jacob.

"Sometimes I . . . don't want to think about mine," said Jonah, looking upset.

Jacob smiled. "But it's nice when they visit us, isn't it?"

A little startled, Jonah whispered, "Do you think my mother knows we're talking about her?"

"Remember," said Jacob, "she's dead, not gone."

"Your parents must have been special," said Jonah.

"Parents are special who make their children feel *they* are special," said Jacob.

"Better than others?" asked Jonah.

"Better about themselves," said Jacob.

"With me here, you must pretend you're a parent. How do you feel about that?" asked Jonah defensively.

"The challenge in parenting is to be who we would have our children become," said Jacob.

"What about how much time I'm taking from you?"

"Parenting is sacred," said Jacob, "and the creation of anything sacred doesn't begin with the question what will I receive from this effort but rather what am I prepared to give."

"I still think your parents must have been great," said Jonah.

"Good parents know that greatness is in each of us, waiting to be born," said Jacob, poking Jonah's chest hintingly.

Embrace Yourself
by Releasing Your Fears

Jonah and Jacob lay in their beds, thinking.

"Jacob," asked Jonah across the dimness, "are you ever afraid of the dark?"

"The darkness illuminates our fears," said Jacob.

"How can the darkness be a light?"

"It shows you your fears," said Jacob.

"Then it is a trap!" stated Jonah, sitting up in his bed.

"We are the trap," said Jacob.

"How is that?" asked the boy.

"All of us have caught ourselves being afraid," said Jacob. "All of us, at some point, have taken our fears to bed with us."

"But, Jacob, even you?"

"*All* of us take our fears to bed with us," said Jacob. "Especially when we grow up."

"Then how do grown-ups ever fall asleep?"

"By remembering," said Jacob, closing his eyes, "that even our fears need their rest."

Even _Me_

Jacob and Jonah looked at each other over the rim of the cups that held their morning tea. Frost had left webs of crystallized ice in the corners of the windows.

"Jacob," asked the boy, "is my being in the bakery a burden to everybody?"

"Who among us is not sometimes a burden to others?" answered Jacob.

"Even you, Jacob?"

"Even _me_," said Jacob.

Take a Teacher—
They Are Everywhere

Along the banks of the river, tufts of grass stuck their fingers through the snow, tenacious against the cold, beckoning the spring. Birds, alive with their chatter, were on the wing and peppering the still shadowy sky.

Jacob and Jonah, turning past the trunk of a guardian oak, were on the way to the bakery when a slim middle-aged woman stepped before them. She adjusted her gloves as if preparing to set the world straight.

"Well! We finally meet," she said with a smile.

Jacob and Jonah looked at each other warily.

"This must be Jonah," the woman observed, friendly and unashamed. The rising sun lent gold to the chestnut color of her braided hair.

"I am," said the boy, looking again to Jacob. "And this is Jacob."

"Yes, I know," she said, meeting Jacob's gaze and smoothing her skirt.

"We're on the way to the bakery," Jacob commented haltingly.

"And I'm on the way to school," said the woman purposefully.

"This is Ruth, the community's new teacher," said Jacob to Jonah.

"So you do know me?" she said.

"That is a large question," answered Jacob, smiling, "but yes, I do. The children who come to see me after school have said that you are a good and kind teacher."

"And I am told that you are wise," said Ruth, her tone softening.

"Those who are wise *take* a teacher," replied Jacob.

"Why don't you walk to the bakery with us?" invited Jonah.

"No," said the woman, her voice dutiful now, "but I should like *you* to come to school with *me*."

"But I am learning from Jacob at the bakery," said Jonah, pouting.

"You can still learn from Jacob," reassured the teacher. "We *all* do."

The sun had risen higher, and the three stood together in a channel of light. Timing is the world set to God's pace, thought Jacob. He recalled the parents who had become suspicious when their children came and sat on the flour sacks to hear his stories. He now understood how hard it was for a parent to release a child to a teacher. How much easier it had been for him to be more wise than understanding.

Jacob took the boy gently by the shoulders. "Jonah, I believe Ruth is correct; go with her now, and come to the bakery after school."

"I will bring him myself," said Ruth, relieved.

"But, Jacob," protested the boy, "I was sent to learn from you."

"Yes," said Jacob, "and I was sent to learn from you!"

"I don't understand, and I *won't* go!" The boy stomped his foot.

"And I didn't understand until now," said Jacob.

"Jacob," persisted Jonah, "what can she teach me?"

"That is for you to discover."

Love Study;
Study Love

When Jacob arrived at the bakery, he found Samuel on his knees trying to put a flame to the pilot light.

"The wind last night," said Samuel, explaining.

Samuel looked around. "Where's Jonah?"

"Ruth, the new teacher, met us on the way," answered Jacob, tearing open the seam of a flour sack. "He went to school with her."

"Went to school?" Samuel made no attempt to mask his disappointment. "But we learned *here*. You learned here. *You're* a teacher."

"Though the bakery may be a good teacher," said Jacob, "what I have learned is that the boy needs a father as much as he needs a teacher."

"Can't you, of all people, be both?" persisted Samuel.

Jacob watched a cloud of flour rise above the mixing bowl as the stirring arm began its endless turning.

"A teacher loves teaching. A father teaches love. Teaching, I know. Loving, I'm learning," answered Jacob.

Many Lovers Share a Bed Without Love

Samuel returned to Jacob's side as he worked at the bread bench. "Jacob, excuse me for wondering, but I was thinking about our earlier conversation and wondering: How does a person learn about love?"

"By loving," said Jacob.

"That doesn't make sense," said Samuel.

"Neither does the fact that many lovers share a bed without love," said Jacob.

"But what if someone has never been in love?" asked Samuel. "Where does he begin?"

"All love is an act of faith," said Jacob, "though faith is not always in fashion. Some of us are fortunate to be warmed by the sun. Others of us must draw our warmth from the faith that *if* there is shadow somewhere, there is sun."

Years Fly;
Days Crawl

For Jacob, the rhythm of work in the bakery was a cadence, familiar and constant. He did not forget where he was, but neither was he fully there. In losing himself, he found his way.

"Jacob!" A sharp voice scratched at his calm.

Jacob remained internal and silent. He was focusing on the way the bakery pans fit together; in them, he saw the interlocking of moments. The stacking of time. The generations. Years fly; days crawl, thought Jacob.

"Jacob!" The voice, brittle and insistent, belonged to an elderly woman.

Jacob looked at the woman without saying anything.

"Young man, are you listening?"

"Yes," said Jacob, smiling. "Are you?"

"Never mind," snapped the woman. "Do you know why I am here?"

"To ask questions, like the rest of us," said Jacob.

"To get answers," said the woman, losing patience.

"It sounds like you already have the answers," said Jacob.

"No," said the woman, grudgingly. "That's why I have come to see you."

"And what could I possibly tell a person of your experience that you don't already know?" asked Jacob.

The woman snorted.

"On the other hand," said Jacob, "sometimes we don't need to know new things but to know in a new way."

The bakery, with its circus of activity and odors, surged around Jacob and the lady.

"Jacob, the reason I have come to see you is because I am upset by the actions of someone who has been a friend over a lifetime."

"Perhaps you ought to let your feelings rest. Friendships, like music, need silences."

"But this is very troubling."

"Most of what we hold that troubles us," said Jacob, "has more to do with how we are holding than what we are holding."

The woman followed Jacob as he moved from the mixer to the scales to weigh out the ingredients for a new dough.

"This friend has broken my trust. It is something I will never, never be able to forget."

"Even when we can't forget," said Jacob, "remember to forgive."

"Why?" asked the old woman.

"Because our books of wisdom remind us that we are to pursue justice but to love mercy."

"And if I cannot find the strength to conduct myself in this way?"

"Then you will understand," said Jacob, "why mercy is the greater justice."

When We Offer Others Harbor,
We Calm Our Own Storms

After dinner, Jacob and Jonah sat by the fire. Jonah spread his schoolbooks on the floor. "We were studying poetry today in school," said Jonah. "And one of the poets wrote that beauty is truth. What do you think, Jacob?"

"I think that the truth has its own poetry, and beauty is not always beautiful."

"Are poets dishonest?"

"More imperfect than dishonest. Like the rest of us."

The boy looked adrift. "Does this mean that all of us grow up to be failures?"

"No," answered Jacob, assuredly, "because all of us can learn and grow from our failures."

"Can't a man drown in his failure?"

"A man can drown in the sea of success, too," said Jacob.

"I will try to be a good sailor," said Jonah, mustering courage.

"Good," said Jacob, "and I will be your harbor."

"And I will be strong," the boy said, though his eyes hinted of tears. Vulnerable now, he asked what he did not want to ask: "To be my harbor—is that enough for you Jacob?"

"It is enough," said Jacob.

"Are you sure?" asked Jonah.

"Yes," said Jacob. "When we offer others harbor, we calm our own storms."

Our Path Has a Purpose
Beyond Where It Leads

In the middle of the day, Jacob took time to rest. He sat on an overturned crate propped against the back door of the bakery. Below the loading dock, he could see footprints left in the mud. Rainwater had filled the outline of each imprint, and pigeons dipped their beaks into the small pools. Our trail is a well, thought Jacob. Others draw water from where we have been. Our path has a purpose beyond where it leads.

"Jacob," asked a woman, wearing her sadness as she approached, "may I take a moment of your time?"

"My time is not mine," said Jacob, and laughed. "Only God owns. The rest of us rent.

"Come sit next to me." Jacob motioned to the woman. "Put your face in the sun, and the world will seem brighter."

"My mother is dying," said the woman as she sat down next to Jacob.

Jacob said nothing.

"She is in such pain. I don't know whether to pray for her to hold on or to let go."

Jacob held to his silence, allowing the woman to arrange her feelings.

"Maybe she can't go because I won't let her. Is that it? Is my love holding her here in pain?"

"Parents learn to hold. And then struggle to hold on," said Jacob. "Children ask to be let go. And then struggle to let go."

"Oh, Jacob," moaned the woman, "why is there so much pain in life?"

"Would the answer to that question make it hurt less?" answered Jacob.

"I keep asking you questions," said the woman, using one hand to clutch the other, "and all you say is 'maybe' and 'perhaps.' I don't want to know what I am feeling. I want to know what to do!" The woman began sobbing.

"Be cautious of knowing more and feeling less," said Jacob. "To find the path ahead take the path within."

"How do I begin?" asked the woman.

"Quietly," said Jacob.

The woman calmed. "My mother is not going to recover. Things are never going to be the same again. Are they?" She stared at Jacob like someone who was standing on a dock watching a ship containing everything she owned drift away.

"You are right," said Jacob. "Nothing will be the same again. Time is not a locked room but an endless hallway. In every moment there is a door."

"And when my mother dies, what then?" asked the woman.

Jacob looked past the woman and across the river toward his cottage. "Though we often think we are alone, we are never as alone as we think."

None of Us Have a Map;
All of Us Have a Compass

When Jacob returned home, Jonah was laying out plates for the evening meal. A slice of the new moon already curled in the window frame.

"How is school?" asked Jacob.

"I like Ruth," answered Jonah.

"I ask you about school, and you tell me you like your teacher. Now, tell me what you learned today."

"Today Ruth taught us about the principles of a compass," said Jonah. "She said that even if a person doesn't know where they are going, they should know how to get there."

Jacob, grinning, his eyes wrinkled, said, "Our books of wisdom tell us that if you don't know where you are going, *any* path will take you there."

"She also said that the compass always points in one direction, toward magnetic north, and that we only know the other compass points from where they stand in relationship to this constant."

"Yes," said Jacob, "and each of us would be wise to pause in our lives and ask what is our magnetic north.

"For some of us," Jacob continued, "our magnetic north is love, for some of us it is fear, for some of us it is power. If love is our magnetic north, we will embrace our experiences with caring and support. If fear is our magnetic north, then we will be ruled by insecurity and doubt. If power is our magnetic north, then control and worry about who is in charge will fill our life. Whatever is our magnetic north is the veil through which we see the world."

"But what about true north? Where is that?"

"It is where we know we *should* be heading."

"But what if you don't know that or are lost?" asked Jonah, a bit disheartened.

"How can we be lost?" asked Jacob. "There are only two doors. We are brought in one and taken out the other. Along the way, whether we know it or not, we are always giving ourselves directions. And while none of us have a map, all of us have a compass."

"Ruth is a good teacher," said Jonah after a pause, and looked to Jacob for agreement.

"Yes," said Jacob, "good teachers are mirrors that are also windows. They allow us to look at ourselves and see the world."

And a Little Child Shall Lead Them

Some members of the community came to Jacob's home to ask his advice. Jacob answered the door with Jonah at his shoulder.

"Jacob," the question pounced on him, "we are concerned about the souls of these homeless people passing through our village and asking for charity."

"The sages," said Jacob, "wrote that most of us think of the other man's soul and our stomach when we should instead be thinking of the other man's stomach and our own soul."

"Well," said another voice, "why can't these people just get jobs like the rest of us?"

"That is their question," said Jacob.

"But if we give them money," complained a man, "they'll just ask for more."

"Which of *us* wants less?" asked Jacob.

"You make it sound like we're no better than they are," said a woman.

"It is not which of us is better," said Jacob, "but whether *we* are good."

"Jacob," said the leader, "you know we want to do the right thing. How do we find our way on these issues?"

"When our mind goes in circles," said Jonah, stepping forward, "our heart offers us a compass."

"What do you know?" asked an indignant older man. "You're just a child."

"And a little child shall lead them," said Jacob.

When I Grow Up

"Jacob," announced Jonah, before bed, "when I grow up, I'm going to be just like you."

"I would remind you," said Jacob, "that when your life is examined in heaven, you will not be asked why you were not more like Jacob but why you were not more as Jonah."

"But I want others to respect me like they respect you."

"Respect yourself. That is something that no one can give you."

"You don't make it sound easy," said Jonah, clearly tired and ready for sleep.

"Life isn't easy," said Jacob, rolling back the covers on the boy's bed, "and I didn't make it."

When We Offer Others a Hand
We Are Lifted

As Jacob bent over to say good night, Jonah spoke, trying to sound older. "Jacob, when I grow up, I will take care of you."

Jacob patted Jonah's hand. "All I ask," said Jacob, "is that one day you will show your children the caring that I have shown you."

"But you have done so much for me," said Jonah.

"When we offer others a hand," said Jacob, "we are lifted."

To Witness a Revolution,
Look at the World Differently

A young man of great seriousness met Jacob on the way to the bakery.

"I am going to change the world," said the fellow, inflating his importance.

"That is not so difficult," said Jacob, continuing on his way.

"Not difficult!" said the young man. "Well, how would you do it?"

"To witness a revolution," said Jacob, "look at the world differently."

"But I have a message that must be heard," insisted the fellow.

"The word *prophet*," said Jacob, holding his pace, "is created from the two words *before speaking*. A true prophet is someone who spends more time listening to God than speaking for God."

Reason Is Its Own Superstition

A professor came to see Jacob with the single intention of showing his mind superior to the simple baker's. They stood next to the ovens and talked.

"I have studied with the greatest teachers," said the man.

"And what have you learned?" asked Jacob.

"I have learned to think with reason," said the professor.

"Reason is its own superstition," said Jacob.

"What do you mean?" challenged the professor.

"We decide what we will believe, then create a system of beliefs to support what we believe," answered Jacob.

"What makes you say that?" asked the man.

"It stands to reason," answered Jacob.

When You're Hungry, Eat;
When You're Done, Wash Your Dish

"Jacob," said Jonah while he swept the floor one morning before school, "sometimes I don't want to do what you say."

Jacob said nothing.

"Aren't you going to argue with me?"

Jacob still said nothing.

Jonah stopped sweeping.

Jacob held to his silence.

"You're making me angry," said the boy.

"Ah," said Jacob, "and to think of all the things you *could* make of yourself."

"Well," said Jonah, with an air of rebellion, "I think the floor is clean enough." Then he lay down his broom and sat on the bed with his arms crossed.

Jacob thought for a moment and then went over and picked up the broom and began sweeping.

"What are you doing?" asked Jonah.

"Sweeping," answered Jacob without anger.

"You aren't going to try and make me do it?" asked the boy.

"Forcing faith is not the force of faith," answered Jacob.

Jonah looked at Jacob cautiously. "I think I understand, but is this some sort of trick to make me do what you want? Like washing the dishes."

Jacob laughed and then said, "Let me tell you a story that was long ago told to me.

"Once there was a man who traveled a great distance to see a wise teacher. When the man at last arrived, he asked the sage, 'What is the nature of truth?'

" 'Have you eaten?' asked the teacher.

" 'No,' said the man. And the teacher gave him something to eat.

"When the man had finished eating, he again asked the teacher, 'What is the nature of truth?'

" 'Are you now done eating?' asked the teacher.

" 'Yes,' answered the man, exasperated, 'but what is the nature of truth?'

" 'When you are hungry,' answered the teacher, 'eat! When you are done, wash your dish!' "

Patience Is Worth the Wait

A lady who was pregnant called to Jacob one day as he carried bread to the front of the bakery.

"Jacob," she asked, rubbing her stomach, "what am I going to have? A boy or a girl?"

Jacob set the loaves down, laughing. "From a prophet you get predictions. From a baker you get bread."

The woman returned his laugh. "Well, I'm getting tired of waiting."

"I think the lesson for parents," said Jacob, "is to get used to waiting. Patience is worth the wait."

Caring Is Praying

A young woman, her voice dreamy, came up to Jacob as he pulled a sack of flour toward the mixer.

"Can I worship God through love?" asked the woman.

"Love," said Jacob, "is a form of worship, but do not worship love."

"Prayer is a way of loving God, isn't it?"

"Loving others is a way of praying to God," said Jacob. "And caring for others is God's prayer for us."

To Fuel Passion
Sometimes You Must Chop Wood

Jacob was preparing to leave the bakery. As he exited, a husband and wife approached him. Though the couple stood next to each other, their bodies suggested a gulf between them.

The wife began. "My husband and I have been married a long time, but . . ."

"No matter what I do for her, it is never enough!" interrupted the husband.

"And he does little enough," countered the wife.

Jacob thought of the quiet meal he and Jonah would share that evening.

"Do you love going to work in the morning?" asked Jacob of the man.

"No," said he.

"But you go?" asked Jacob.

"Of course he goes," answered the wife.

"Why?" asked Jacob.

"Because if you don't work, you don't eat," answered the husband.

"Marriage is a banquet," said Jacob, "but you have to put food on the table."

"So," asked the man, "marriage is like going to work?"

"No," said Jacob. "All I am saying is that marriages don't work without work."

"And what about romance?" asked the wife.

"To fuel passion you must sometimes chop wood," said Jacob.

Manners Reflect

Jonah returned home from school, exasperated. "Why," asked Jonah, "do I have to be polite?"

"Excuse me," said Jacob.

"I asked, 'Why do I have to be polite?' "

"I heard you the first time," said Jacob. "I was just trying to be polite so you could hear yourself."

"Manners are ridiculous," said the boy.

"Manners reflect," said Jacob. "They allow others to see what you think of them and allow them a glimpse of you."

Confidence and Doubt
Are Equally Contagious

Jonah slammed shut his schoolbooks, making a statement. "When I get older, I'm going to be rich," said the boy.

"Want less and you are already rich," said Jacob.

"You don't believe me, do you?"

"Confidence and doubt are equally contagious," said Jacob, putting down his cup of tea.

Jonah looked around the small room where the two of them sat. "Jacob, wouldn't you like to have more than what you have?"

"Over time," said Jacob, "we are richer for what we discover we don't need than for getting what we thought we wanted."

Making the World Whole

Ruth was waiting for Jacob as he stepped from the bakery. In her eyes were sparks of purpose.

"I'm upset with you, Jacob," said Ruth, wasting little time in making her point. "Jonah often speaks as if God were a man. I've noticed you have the same habit."

"When I'm referring to God the Father," answered Jacob.

"But clearly you also see God as a woman?" Ruth's eyes remained on target.

"When She lets me see Her," replied Jacob.

"Oh," said Ruth, half laughing. "And do you see Her here?" She pointed to the surrounding woods.

"Why do you ask?" said Jacob. "Are you going to show me where God isn't?"

Ruth remained wary. "I still feel you are avoiding my question."

"We are all God's children," said Jacob. "The issue is language, not spiritual. We are an expression of God and not the other way around."

"But you certainly don't hesitate in speaking for *Him*."

"I don't speak for Him *or* Her," said Jacob, "because I do not see God divided into two."

Ruth was thinking.

When Jacob continued, his voice was more tender than teaching. "There is a learning from long ago that prior to our birth we are both male and female, and after we are born, we spend our life trying to find our complement. That search continues today. *All* of us are looking not only for our partner but for that lost part inside of us."

"And what happens when we find our lost half?" asked Ruth.

"When we find our other half, we make our world whole," said Jacob, holding his look to hers.

Hold Power by Letting Go

"Jacob," said Jonah, washing the dishes after dinner, "I know that people think you are wise, but doesn't it bother you that other men think they are more important than you?"

"People who think they are more important than others have forgotten what is important," said Jacob. "I'm a man of faith. Faith holds power by letting go."

"So you don't mind bending to what others want you to do?" asked the boy.

"To bend is not to bow," answered Jacob.

"But being strong is what it means to be a man." Jonah's voice stressed the word *man*.

"Every man has strengths," said Jacob. "And every strength is its own weakness."

Mornings Are Wiser Than Evenings

"It's time for bed," said Jacob to Jonah.

The boy moved slowly, to Jacob's frustration.

"Did you hear me?" asked Jacob.

"I heard you," said Jonah. "But does it make you mad when I don't listen to you?"

"I try to think about how many times I haven't listened to me," said Jacob.

"And I'm tired of you always having *just* the right thing to say."

"You're just tired."

"I'm tired of you."

"Me too, sometimes," said Jacob.

"So why don't you stop answering everyone's questions?"

"Should I start with this one?"

"Jacob!"

"What?"

"You're frustrating me."

"What's frustrating you is you."

"So what's your suggestion?"

"Go to bed. Mornings are wiser than evenings."

"That's an old saying."

"Yes," said Jacob, "but at the moment you're not making me feel any younger."

Time Does Not So Much Create
as Unveil

And now for Jacob, Jonah, and the world that lived on the river that ran through their village, years passed.

Jacob, still in bed, felt the world turn beneath him. Perhaps, thought Jacob, I am not too old, but it is later. Without opening his eyes, he slowed his breathing. Weightless and ageless, he entered the familiar stream of prayer.

Moments later, Jacob felt the morning sun on his face and opened his eyes. Dawn was painted across the window.

Jonah came into the room and shook Jacob's shoulder lightly. Jacob could feel the strength in the hand upon him.

"Remember me?" asked Jonah, smiling. "I was the little boy who arrived yesterday."

"Who can remember that far back?" said Jacob, teasing.

Jonah's smile broadened. "Jacob the Baker says: 'Reality is only a memory ahead of its time.' "

At the table it was Jonah who raised the bread in prayer before they broke the morning's fast.

"Ruth has asked me to help her by teaching the younger students," said Jonah.

"Yes," said Jacob. "And what will you teach them?"

"That learning begins with listening." Jonah was interrupted by a quiet but clear knock at the door. Neither of the men seemed surprised.

Jonah quickly went to the door and welcomed Ruth in. Jacob offered her the chair next to his.

Ruth placed her hand on Jacob's, in a small intimacy. "I am cold, and you are so warm," she said.

"Even when you are cold, you are warm," said Jacob.

"Thank you, Jacob," said Ruth, retrieving her hand. "Kindness is warmer than wisdom."

Jonah had helped Ruth take off her cloak. While he hung it near the fire, he turned and looked back at Jacob and Ruth sitting next to each other sharing their morning tea.

Love is magic, thought Jonah. It turns one and one into One.

Jacob's Ladder

In the middle of the night a heavy rain began to fall. After several hours, the tired roof on Jacob's home began to leak.

"Jacob," said Jonah. "I'll go up the ladder and cover the shingles."

"I will hold the ladder," said Jacob, and followed Jonah from the house.

As they stepped outside, the storm was retreating. A bright moon peered through the fleeing clouds. Jacob braced himself at the ladder's footing while Jonah began the climb.

At the top, Jonah disappeared onto the roof, and Jacob waited, expecting Jonah's return at any moment.

"Are you all right?" shouted Jacob.

"I'm fine, and if the rain returns I think we'll stay dry," said Jonah. He peered over the roof's edge. "There's an incredible view from up here."

"Often what makes a view incredible is the viewer," said Jacob, stepping onto the ladder. "Wait there. I will join you."

"Now, you be careful!" said Jonah.

Jacob began the climb, minding each foot as he stepped on the rungs. At the top, he stopped.

Jonah rested on the roof and stared at the rapidly clearing sky. "The stars look like they've been washed by the rain."

"Perhaps," said Jacob, "that is the way God bathes the world."

"Do you think," asked Jonah, "that it was on a night like this that Jacob in the Bible saw angels on the ladder from heaven?"

"Same heaven," said Jacob.

"I guess the difference is that Jacob was in the wilderness," said Jonah.

"Sometimes," said Jacob, "it's not until we're around others that we feel alone and in the wild."

"Yes," said Jonah, "but Jacob *was* alone."

"Jacob only thought he was alone."

"Because he had angels for company?"

"Because he had God for company. The angels were messengers."

"And what was the message?"

"The message," said Jacob, "is that between heaven and earth there is a ladder."

Jacob began his descent. Jonah stood and moved to the ladder. Halfway down, the two stopped and looked up. The moon held them in channels of light.

"What about the angels?" asked Jonah, returning his gaze to the stars. "Where are they?"

"They," said Jacob, "are any of us who use the ladder."

"But the angels," said Jonah, now looking at Jacob. "Weren't they coming down as well as going up?"

"Yes," said the baker. "And that is Jacob's ladder. While it connects us to heaven, it also brings heaven to earth."

"Then love is also a ladder," said Jonah.

"Without love," said Jacob, setting his foot on the ground, "we cannot climb out of ourselves."

Coincidence Is God's Cloak of Humility

Outside the bakery, the storm of the night before had left a calm in its wake. The cold bright light of an early spring was in the air. Inside, Jacob was walking to the front of the bakery carrying long loaves of bread in his arms as if they were sheaves of wheat.

Samuel took the load from Jacob and set the loaves in a basket.

"Jacob, the spiritual leader from our neighboring village had to spend the night among us because of the bad weather. He is a respected man of God. He would like to see you."

"So look at me. I'm here," said Jacob, appraising himself from head to toe.

"You don't understand," said Samuel, concerned by Jacob's casual attitude. "He's changed his *plans* to meet you."

"My mother used to say, 'If you want to give God a good laugh, tell Him your plans,' " said Jacob.

"Listen, Jacob, I will let you use the corner of the bakery where I sit to do my paperwork. You will be less disturbed. I will bring him to you." He then moved an unsure Jacob toward a chair and left.

Jacob watched Samuel leave. And waited.

"Jacob?"

The man behind the voice was dressed entirely in dark clothing and extended his hand in greeting.

Jacob stood up and took his hand, then both men sat for a moment in silence. The visitor finally spoke.

"Jacob, you make me feel . . . comfortable."

"We usually make ourselves comfortable or uncom-fortable," said Jacob quietly.

"Jacob," began the man with a tone of confession, "my entire life has been in the pursuit and service of the spiritual. Since I have been a child, I have been drawn to this life. But something has changed. I feel that either I have abandoned God or God has abandoned me."

"And," said Jacob feigning seriousness, "would you like my help in finding God, or shall I help God find you?"

The man laughed.

"Good," said Jacob.

"I laugh and you say, 'Good.' Why?" asked the man.

"Because," said Jacob, "too often people who are trying to find God begin by losing their sense of humor."

The man waved his hands at the bakery behind him. "Jacob, can you see God even here?"

"There was a great teacher," said Jacob, "who reminded us that God hides Himself in His manifestations and shows Himself in his concealments."

"And the storm, my coming to visit you?" asked the man. "Can you see God in that? Or is that only coincidence?"

"There was another great teacher," said Jacob, "who reminded us that coincidence is God's way of remaining anonymous."

"But *you*, Jacob," said the man. "What do you think?"

"I think," said Jacob, pulling on his beard, "that we are a reflection of God. While others may look at the world around them and see only coincidence, I look at the world and see coincidence as God's cloak of humility."

"But what would you do if God were to abandon you?" asked the man carefully.

"Then I would be wise to remember that it is my own vision, and not God, that has left me," said Jacob.

"Jacob," asked the man, shaking his head, "are you always wrapped in God's cloak of humility?"

"Oh no," said Jacob, smiling. "Even God sometimes takes off His cloak."

"And when we witness God's hand in a coincidence, is that what you call a miracle?"

"Long ago," said Jacob, "I reminded myself that what makes a miracle is our willingness to see one."

The man stood and prepared to leave. "Jacob," he said, "I will tell others about you."

"The less said, the more heard," said Jacob.

Speak Softly;
Listen Loudly

The day was erased by dusk. Preparing to leave, Samuel observed Jacob sweeping a corner of the bakery.

While Jacob swept, his head was cocked to one side as if he were straining to hear the notes in a distant concert.

"Other men sweep, Jacob, you dance. How is that?"

There was no response.

Samuel continued, "I know you are not sweeping. You can tell *me*. What are you really doing?"

Jacob laughed. "What I am really doing is sweeping; what I am also really doing is raking the paths in the Garden of Eden."

"And who gave you this job?"

"No one gives you your work," said Jacob. "You find your own work. And often the hardest labor is in the looking."

Samuel pushed further.

"Don't you think it's a little strange, Jacob, to be in a bakery and working in the Garden of Eden at the same time?"

"And which job should I give up?" asked Jacob.

"That is not what I meant," answered Samuel quickly.

Jacob smiled. "Samuel, you may have noticed we're getting a little older. When we were younger, we thought we could move heaven and earth. Now my efforts are simply to find a little heaven *on* earth."

"And so you have found some heaven?" asked Samuel.

"In life, less is lost than we have hidden," answered Jacob.

"And God helped you find it?" Samuel laughed.

"No," answered Jacob, with all seriousness, "but He taught me how to ask for directions."

"And how do you do that?" asked Samuel.

"Speak softly; listen loudly," said Jacob.

Life Is Lived Forward
and Understood Backward

Jacob approached his home in the darkness. Through the window he could see Ruth and Jonah reviewing a lesson. A fire sparked in the hearth. Smoke coiled out the tin chimney and across the slanted roof. Jacob heard himself repeating the line he had memorized as a boy but only now understood. "And the Lord God said: 'It is not good that the man should be alone. It is not good that the man should be alone.'"

As Jacob entered, the two faces turned and embraced him with a single smile. The light from the candles cast mountain ranges rising and falling across their cheeks. The corners of the room softened. A man can be at home with himself, thought Jacob, but that is very different from being home.

"It is late," said Ruth.

"Yes," said Jacob. "Samuel wanted to talk with me."

"I'm glad you were not alone," said Ruth.

Jacob wondered how she knew what he was thinking.

After washing and prayers, the three sat down to eat. As Jonah dipped a thick slice of bread into his soup and began to ask a question, Jacob realized suddenly how the boy's voice had deepened and his shoulders had broadened. Time, thought Jacob. Boys become men while men struggle to be men.

"Jacob," asked Jonah, "why is the Bible, in Hebrew, called The Law?"

Ruth looked up.

Resting the side of his head and beard against his open hand, Jacob responded, "Because, like the law that says when we jump up we fall down, The Law is the truth observed. To be *observant* is a sacred responsibility."

"In other words," said Jonah, "following The Law is another way of paying attention to the universe."

"Just as watching the world is a way of keeping an eye out for God," said Jacob.

"But to understand the universe is impossible," exclaimed Jonah.

"That doesn't keep us from observing it," said Jacob, "or from using the stars to help us find our way."

"So is it a sin not to be observant?" asked Jonah, only half joking.

"It is a sin to ignore others or the world around us," corrected Ruth.

The warmth in the room had now caused the windows to fog. When Jacob spoke, his voice was edged with caring. "Love is the beginning and ending of all learning. The Hebrew word for *heart* begins with the last letter of the Bible and ends with the first letter in the Bible."

"Why is it backward?" asked Jonah.

"Because," said Jacob, "life is lived forward but understood backward. We arrive at the end of our learning only to discover what has been true from the beginning."

Ruth's eyes shone with respect. "Jacob you are a true teacher."

"It is you and Jonah who are the great teachers," said Jacob. "For by your company, God has been kind to me. And anyone who can not learn from kindness is a fool."

A Love Beyond Love

The house had grown still. Night reigned. But sleep did not come to either Jacob or Jonah.

"Jacob?" Jonah half whispered, hoping Jacob was awake.

"Yes," said Jacob, pleased to have the company.

"I have a question that has been bothering me for a long time."

Jacob remembered the boy behind the man's voice.

"Why," asked Jonah, "did God want Abraham to sacrifice Isaac?"

"I think God wanted Abraham's struggle, not Isaac's sacrifice," said Jacob.

"What was Abraham struggling with?"

"To love God."

"And God felt Abraham needed this lesson?"

"I think God felt we would need it."

"Why?"

"So we could understand that to love God is a love beyond love."

"Is that *so* hard to understand?"

"I didn't think so, until you came to live with me."

"Me?"

"Yes. From your being here I learned that to love God we need a reference. The story of Abraham and Isaac is the story of love between a father and his child. These feelings are profound and pure and timeless.

And from these feelings we may *begin* to understand the depths of spiritual love."

"What an incredible conflict God's demand must have presented Abraham," said Jonah.

"We are only as strong as what we struggle with," said Jacob.

"Would you have done the same thing as Abraham?" asked Jonah.

"My job is to learn from the story. Abraham was a patriarch. I am a baker."

"You know, Jacob," said Jonah, "you never seem to suffer from pride in your answers."

"Only those who suffer from pride deny its presence," said Jacob.

"Would it upset you," asked Jonah, "if I told you I want you to be proud of me one day?"

"I am proud of you this day," said Jacob.

"Do I sound foolish asking you this?"

Jonah's earnestness cut through the darkness.

"Sincerity is its own truth," said Jacob. "To be proud is not necessarily to suffer from pride."

Jacob shut his eyes and heard himself praying not for what he wanted but for what he did not want to lose.

Forgetting Can Be a Higher Form of Love Than Forgiving

A habit of several years, Jacob walked with Jonah toward school. Jonah now helped Ruth with the classes. Jacob noted that the shadow falling ahead of them was not of a boy and a man but of two men.

In youth, thought Jacob, we are always asking: When? As we grow older we find ourselves asking: So soon?

"Jacob," said Jonah, with some hesitancy, "in a book I am reading, the author has written that isolation leads to intimacy. Can you explain what this means?"

"Perhaps the author means that we fill our lives with noise and motion and the company of others to distract ourselves," said Jacob. "For most of us, these are habits we do not examine, although the cost of these habits is that we lack self-intimacy. We live alone in a crowd and refuse to visit ourselves."

"Sad," said Jonah.

"What's more sad," said Jacob, "is that when we can't embrace ourselves, we have a difficult time embracing others."

A cold wind blew, and Jacob pulled his jacket closer.

"But that means," said Jonah, "if we want to enjoy the company of others, we need to spend time alone."

"I know that sounds like a contradiction," said Jacob, "but look around you. Life pushes when it pulls. God marries the opposites: life and death; night and day; man and woman. In their contradiction is their fit."

"But often the opposites fight," said Jonah.

"Jonah, the world is whole. When opposites fight they are often struggling to fit."

Jonah smiled. "In this world of opposites, you once said: 'Wisdom is a work of art sculpted from our ignorance.' "

Jacob's smile met Jonah's. "Do you remember everything I say?"

"No," answered Jonah. "You also once said: 'Sometimes forgetting can be a higher form of love than forgiving.' "

We Are Shopkeepers
Selling Ourselves What We Want to Hear

A businessman's purposeful stride brought him next to Jacob on the way to the bakery.

"Jacob, people tell me that you *always* have something clever to say."

"Only a fool is always clever," answered Jacob, maintaining his pace.

The man grinned but quickly found himself falling behind. "Please, Jacob," he said, hurrying to catch up, "what can you tell me about the business of living?"

"We are shopkeepers selling ourselves what we want to hear," said Jacob, speaking over his shoulder.

"Look, Jacob," said the man as he drew even, "what I know is money. The cost of any investment is always judged against what it could be making for you invested somewhere else. On these terms, what is the economics of self?" He smiled at the cleverness of his own question.

"The cost of being who you are at any moment is not being who you might be," said Jacob. "That is the economics of self."

"So it might cost a man a great deal not to be what he might become?"

"Clearly you do understand economics," said Jacob.

The man laughed. "And what kind of investor am I?"

"A man who is hesitant to invest in what he might become," answered Jacob.

"Why?" asked the man.

"Because," said Jacob, "like most of us, you believe you have a contract to only be who you are now."

"But," said the man, "I don't remember ever making this deal."

"My friend," said Jacob, "none of us do."

Stepping Back
Sometimes Affords Us a Closer View

For several days, an elderly woman had arrived each morning at the bakery. She spent endless hours nursing a cup of tea and staring through a crack in the doorway that separated the customers from the bakery itself. Samuel had been patient with her. When he would brush by her, she would quickly return to work on a small piece of tapestry that sat on her lap.

Then, one afternoon, with no warning, the woman prepared to leave. On seeing this, Samuel's curiosity became an itch that demanded to be scratched, and he caught the woman's attention.

"Are you leaving before talking with him?" he asked.

"With whom?" asked the woman.

"Jacob," said Samuel, confirming what he already knew.

"How did you know?" asked the woman.

"Because who would come to my bakery to buy bread?" moaned Samuel.

"Perhaps I shouldn't bother him with my questions."

"Don't worry," said Samuel. "His own questions disturbed him long before ours ever arrived . . . Jacob said that," admitted the bakery owner.

"Come," said Samuel, guiding the visitor to Jacob, who had his back to them and was bent over the bread bench.

"Jacob," said Samuel, "there is someone who has come to see you." Without waiting for a response, Samuel patted the woman's hand and moved away.

"At last," said Jacob, turning to the woman. "At last my teacher has come to see me."

The woman looked confused.

Jacob looked upon the piece of tapestry in her hands. She clung to its familiar territory.

"There was a great teacher," said Jacob, "who told us that life was like a tapestry."

The woman's eyes listened.

"I wondered about this for a long time," said Jacob. "And then, watching you over the last days, I discovered that one works on a tapestry from the back. That you work on it without seeing the larger pattern. That all you see are the colored stitches running at odds and at angles to each other. That, indeed, is like life: One day is woven into the next. But we cannot see the implication of every stitch in time. And so we work blind. Courage is the required pattern in life. Courage and faith."

The woman looked at Jacob as if she had left the window of her life open a few inches and he, somehow, had seen the bare, illuminated sadness of her rooms.

"I feel overwhelmed," she said, barely speaking. "There *never* seems to be enough time, time just to step *back* and take a look at our lives."

"But that's why God has created a time-out," said Jacob.

"A time-out?"

"Yes," said Jacob. "It is the first law of time. The Sabbath. The Sabbath is a spiritually sanctified time-out. The Sabbath is the concept by which time sets its watch. The Sabbath affords us a perspective, even on time. It is an opportunity to see that our work in life is also a work of art. One day in seven we are to step back and turn our tapestry over."

"And what will we see then?" asked the woman.

"We will see," said Jacob, "that life has two sides, that there are grand patterns in small stitches. Strangely enough, by stepping back from life we sometimes get a closer view."

"Perhaps you are right, Jacob," said the woman, slowly exhaling, "but it is very difficult."

"We become our habits," said Jacob. "It is difficult to pause because it is not in our habit to do so. And when we do, we feel that life is slipping by us, that we are not being responsible, not fully partaking in our joys.

Nevertheless, there is peace in pausing, and only those who pause may begin again."

"Peace," said the woman, as if she were staring at a distant island that held a dreamy allure. "Sometimes peace is a long time coming."

"Yes," said Jacob, "but even the briefest peace is its own blessing. And any blessing that does not bring us peace is no blessing."

To Hear the Truth
You Must Honestly Listen

Ruth met Jacob after work. They walked home together. The sky was filled with a mountain range cloudscape, red in the distance.

"Jacob," said Ruth, "Jonah is getting older, and he is wise beyond his years."

"Oh that we have the character to meet our wisdom," said Jacob playfully.

"Jonah's voice has even begun to sound like yours," said Ruth.

"His silences too?" asked Jacob, smiling.

"Does your voice sound like your father's?" asked Ruth.

"At some point in his life," said Jacob, "every man who listens to himself hears his father."

"What of those who don't know their fathers?"

"At some point in each of our lives we sound like strangers to ourselves."

Ruth laced her arm through Jacob's. "I think Jonah is lucky to have you for a father."

Jacob stopped in his path. He looked into the sky, which had gone black. He began to speak and fought the words, unsure of their emotional depth as they came to him. "Do you really think he sees me as . . ."

Ruth placed her finger on Jacob's lips and said softly, "Better to have feelings without words than words without feeling."

Time Teaches

Jonah walked through the darkened room and touched Jacob's arm while he slept.

Jacob turned and looked into the concern on Jonah's face.

"I had a bad dream," said Jonah. "It was like the kind I used to have when I first came here."

"I remember," said Jacob.

"Some part of me is still afraid," said Jonah.

"It's okay," said Jacob.

"How can you say that?" asked Jonah. "Look at me. I'm a grown man."

"Grown men have grown fears," said Jacob. "Fear is the father of courage, the grandfather of humility, and the patriarch of prayer."

"What do you mean?" asked Jonah.

"A man who cannot face his fears will never find courage," said Jacob. "Fear is a realization that we are not all-powerful. It is a recognition that there is a force beyond us in the universe. Fear, not fear of fear, is a door to humility. And humility is the door to prayer."

"Why did I have to wait until now to learn this lesson?" asked Jonah.

"You didn't," said Jacob. "Most of us don't lack for information. The question is whether we have the character to act on what we know. Our character is our architecture."

"Well, I wish I felt stronger," said Jonah.

"Trust me," said Jacob. "All of us will discover more reasons to be humble than we are seeking. It is a lesson that we learn and forget."

"Why do we keep forgetting?" asked Jonah.

"Because," said Jacob, "we are no sooner humble then we begin to take pride in our humility."

"And this happens to all of us?"

"Pride convinces all of us that it only handicaps others."

"So humility is a lesson that we are constantly learning," said Jonah.

"Oh yes," said Jacob. "Time teaches."

"Good, because I have many more questions," said Jonah.

The River Runs;
It Never Walks.

A morning fog that had covered the village was lifting. Jacob sat on the steps outside at the back of the bakery.

Now that Jonah and Ruth were so much a part of his life, Jacob could touch the aloneness that for so long had been his life. Now that Jonah and Ruth were in his life, intimacy had become part of Jacob's perspective.

Pigeons paraded at Jacob's feet. They looked up at him in anticipation for the crumbs of bread he carried in his pocket. "We expect what we have experienced," said Jacob, pulling crumbs from his coat and spreading them on the ground. The birds rushed to the food, cooing while they ate.

Samuel arrived and stared at his friend. "Are you coming in? Or are you going to sit out there feeding those birds my good bread?"

"I'm going to wait a little while before I come in," said Jacob.

"Perhaps you're waiting for a higher invitation," said Samuel, looking to the heavens.

"God waits with those who are waiting for Him," said Jacob.

"So you're not waiting for God."

"No," said Jacob, "I just wanted to sit here and peel the moment."

"Are you going to offer me a bite?" asked Samuel.

"Help yourself," said Jacob. "Time is an orchard. Every moment is ripe with opportunity."

"I think a few of my moments are past ripe," said Samuel.

Jacob laughed.

"You think I've gone to seed," said Samuel.

"There are orchards in seeds," said Jacob.

"I remember when you first said that."

"Yes," said Jacob, "but in life we never hear the same thing twice."

"Still, life does repeat itself?" asked Samuel.

"Different bends. Same river," said Jacob.

"Well," said Samuel, "it seems to me that it's moving faster."

"The river runs," said Jacob. "It never walks."

To Have a Friend,
Be One

Max approached Jacob with a sack of flour for a new dough. Max dropped the sack at Jacob's feet and stood forward for a moment regarding him.

"You know, Jacob," said Max, "all these people come to you with questions. Finally, I have one."

Jacob lifted his focus.

"Do you know why God made our arms this long?" Max held out his arms in front of him.

"No," said Jacob, at a loss for an answer to the strange question.

"So we could do this," said Max. Then he gave Jacob a hug and walked away.

Friendship, thought Jacob. Simple. Honest. Friendship.

Suffering Happiness

"Jacob," said a young man, following the baker while he worked, "I want to be a writer, but I'm worried that I haven't suffered enough."

"It was a wise man who said, 'I've had a lot of problems in my life and most of them have never happened,'" answered Jacob.

"Then I have nothing to worry about," said the young man, still ill at ease.

"Relax," said Jacob. "Worry finds even those who are not looking for it."

"What about suffering?" asked the young man.

Jacob looked straight into the young man's face. "Many find they do not have the courage to suffer happiness."

Every Diamond
Began as a Piece of Coal

A slight woman positioned herself next to Jacob, making it impossible for him to avoid her. "I feel like I'm under a lot of pressure," said the woman. "Other people don't value me."

"Every diamond began as a piece of coal," said Jacob.

"And what could possibly transform my situation?"

"The same elements that make coal into diamonds," said Jacob. "Pressure and time."

The Wisdom of Laughter

Two friends came to Jacob in the hope he would settle an argument.

"I think we learn more in life through tears," said one woman.

"And I think we learn more through laughter," said the second woman.

"Which of us is right?" they asked in unison.

Jacob laughed.

"Are you laughing at us?" they demanded.

"I'm crying," said Jacob.

"You sure have a funny way of crying," said the first woman.

"That is the wisdom of laughter," said Jacob.

The Most Important Things in Life
Aren't Things

A young man with a pad and pencil approached Jacob while he worked.

"What are the most important things in life?" asked the youth eagerly.

"The most important things in life aren't things," said Jacob.

"Okay, so what do you hold dear?" Again the pencil was ready.

"Not what, who," said Jacob.

The young man scratched his head. "Are you saying that people are the most important things in life?"

"No," said Jacob. "What's most important is not to treat people as things."

On Becoming Young

"Give me some room," rasped an elderly voice. A cane moved through the crowd in the bakery toward Jacob.

"Listen to me, Jacob," said the old man. "Experience is the great teacher."

"Yes," said Jacob, "but the tuition is your life."

"Humph," said the old man, coughing and pursing his lips. "I can certainly see that you're no teacher."

"What we learn from others," said Jacob, "has less to do with seeing others as teachers and more to do with our willingness to be students."

"So," said the man, now sharply eyeing Jacob, "you expect the old to learn from the young?"

"What I hope," said Jacob, "is for the old to remember how young they feel when they continue to learn."

Sunrise, Sunset

It was early twilight. Ruth stood next to Jacob at the foot of the fields that ran to the mountains. Giant rolls of hay, still covered for the winter, punctuated the expanse. For a long time they sat silently enjoying the simple pleasure of each other's company under the open sky.

"Jacob," thought Ruth out loud, "have you noticed how it sometimes is difficult to distinguish between the sky at sunrise and sunset?"

"Yes," said Jacob.

"And your sky, Jacob. Is it at sunrise or sunset?"

"Both," said Jacob.

"How is that possible?"

"Jonah will be leaving soon," said Jacob, listening to the sadness in his own voice. "Jonah's sun is rising. My time with him is setting."

"I believe," said Ruth, taking Jacob's hand in hers, "that you will be in every sunrise of Jonah's life."

"And I believe," said Jacob, looking into the sky reflected in Ruth's eyes, "that you are the sun rising in my life."

When We Help Strangers
We Occasionally Aid Angels

The bright glint of day melted the frost on the windows and filled the room. Jacob had slept late. He moved quickly now, not wanting to miss his appointed rounds at the bakery.

On his hurried way to the bakery, Jacob met an old man with a long white beard. The old man was waiting at the same turn in the path where Jacob had first met Ruth. The stranger asked Jacob if he could point out the way to the school.

Jacob instead offered to walk with him.

"I don't mean to take you out of your way," said the man.

"It is we who are lost when we don't help others to find their way," said Jacob.

The man looked at Jacob curiously. "But I am a stranger."

"When we help strangers," said Jacob, "we occasionally aid angels."

Making the Rules Golden

Outside the school, a breeze blew through the flowers along its unassuming wood walls. Jonah's voice could be heard from an open window.

"And during this period of time," said Jonah, his voice as much that of a storyteller as a teacher, "people carried two pocket watches."

"Why?" asked a girl.

"Because," said Jonah, "watches were inclined to run down, and the first could then be reset from the second watch."

"But why are you telling us this?" asked a boy. "That's the problem with school. We learn things that don't mean anything."

"Oh, but it does," said Jonah, his tone as calm as it was insistent. "People in a community are like these two pocket watches. There comes a time in each of our lives when *each of us* needs support, because we all run down. When that happens, *each of us* needs to count on the people next to us that *they* will lend us the time to rest and reset ourselves."

"I still don't see how people can be like pocket watches!" said the boy, laughing and drawing titters from the other children.

"The moments we share with others," said Jonah, "remind us we are neighbors in time."

"Jonah," asked a girl, "isn't the real message of the watch story that we should be nice to others because we will need them to be nice to us?"

"That is a truth backward as well as forward," said Jonah.

"What do you mean?" asked the girl.

"Do unto others as you would have them do unto you," said Jonah. "Do not do unto others what you would not have them do unto you."

"Jonah, that's just the golden rule." The girl giggled.

"It's *only* a rule," said Jonah. "When we embrace it, it becomes golden."

We Remember to Forget

"Tell us," said one of the schoolchildren to Jonah, "why we should treat our neighbors as ourselves."

"I will tell you a story," said Jonah, quieting the room with the blanket of his voice.

"Once there was only one boy in the whole world. He felt he was the most important person, and he was, because there was no one to argue with him. There was also no one to talk with or play with. So one night, just before falling asleep, he prayed.

" 'Dear God,' said the boy, 'I know that You made me special, but I wonder if You would please make more people just like me.'

"The next day when the boy woke he found that the world was now filled with little boys, and they all looked just like him. They also all felt they were special, just like him.

"Oh no, thought the boy, this won't do at all.

"That night the boy again prayed to God: 'Dear God, please let all the others know that they are not as special as I am.'

"And God answered, 'But how can I make the others think they are less important than you if the others *are* you?

" 'There must be something You can do,' said the boy, upset that he had upset his world.

" 'This is what I will do,' said God. 'I will put everyone in disguise. So though everyone is you, no one will look quite the same, and some will look quite different.'

" 'But that won't be enough,' said the boy. 'Everyone will remember that beneath the surface we are very much the same, that You made us all.'

" 'Trust Me,' said God, 'even you will remember to forget.' "

Prayer Is a Way
of Giving God Company

"Jonah," said a little girl, "you told us a story about a little boy who was lonely, but I was wondering if God was ever lonely."

"Prayer," said Jonah, "is a way of giving God company."

"And if we forget to pray, or don't want to pray?" asked a boy.

"What you want to ask yourself," said Jonah, "is how long you can hold your breath."

"Why?" asked the boy.

"Since each of us is filled with God's breath," said Jonah, "each time we exhale, we are in God's company."

To Everything
There Is a Season

Jonah looked up from the faces of the schoolchildren and saw both Jacob and the old man standing in the doorway. Ruth remained in her chair behind the desk at the head of the room.

"Hello, Jonah," said the visitor.

"Hello, Uncle," said Jonah, surprised. "It's been a long time."

"Yes," said the voice through the white beard. "But the time has come."

Ruth rose from behind the desk and told the children they could go out and play. Some running, but most cautious, they slid past Jacob and the visitor, whispering, stealing looks, and giggling while they exited.

Now the children's laughter from outside framed the silence that momentarily hung in the room. Jonah walked toward the visitor and was greeted with open arms.

Jonah and the old man took a step back from each other as if surveying how time had shifted the geography in their appearance. The sun laid its full face against the window.

"Jacob and Ruth," said Jonah, "this is my uncle. When my grandfather died, my uncle was named to head the Council of Sages."

"Only until Jonah returned," said the old man, raising a finger to make his point. "I promised my brother that I would honor his will. And it was his will for you"—the finger now pointed at Jonah—"to return and take your place at the Chair of the Council when you were ready."

"And do you think I am ready, Uncle?" asked Jonah.

Now the visitor turned to Jacob. "Let me ask the man who has been as a teacher and father to you."

Jacob said nothing. He thought of the evening he had found Jonah at his door. He thought of the bowls of soup they had shared at their simple table when winter howled in the night. He thought of the broadening shoulders he saw in the boy's shadow when they walked to the bakery. He thought of how a father learns to hold a child only to learn how to let go. He thought of what he might say at this moment and found he had no words. Instead, he found tears.

Jonah spoke. "This man," he nodded to Jacob, "has taught me to love wisdom, and the wisdom of love."

Jonah walked to Jacob, and they embraced. The head of each man rested on the other's shoulder.

In a world of words there was much to say. But though nothing was said, everything was heard.

Flowers waved in the wind. Children laughed. The moment froze under the sun.

"I am ready," said Jonah.

Life Has Depths
That Only Time Explores

Samuel found Jacob in a corner of the bakery stacking bread boards. Jacob idly threw cornmeal across the boards and then placed one board on top of the other. A single light hovered above over Jacob in the large room. It would be several hours before others arrived.

"I tell you to come to work later and you arrive earlier," said Samuel.

"The sages say we are not expected to finish the work, but neither are we excused from it," said Jacob, flicking his wrist and fanning the cornmeal across another board.

"I heard that Jonah will be leaving," said Samuel.

"Yes," said Jacob, snapping his wrist again.

"What will you do?" asked Samuel.

"I will do what any person does who says goodbye to a child he has helped to raise," said Jacob. "I will thank God for allowing me the blessing of love, and then I will continue on."

"And your feelings?" asked Samuel.

Jacob stopped what he was doing. He put both hands on the half stack of boards in front of him. "I feel," said Jacob, "like a man who has spent his entire life swimming through a vast body of water. When I was younger and raised my head from my effort, the horizon seemed to forever disappear into the distance. That horizon, before me, no longer grows more distant. It has, in some ways, drawn closer. But what I have discovered is that the water beneath me is deeper than I have ever known."

"Yes," said Samuel, letting his head drop to his chest. "Life has depths that only time explores."

"And time," said Jacob, once again beginning to stack the bakery boards, "time does not wait for us to learn every lesson before it moves on to the next."

We Are Life's Pages

School was over. Jonah walked among the desks. He thought about the hours he had sat here and learned. His finger bounced on the back of the chairs as he passed. He wanted to say goodbye to Ruth but didn't know where to begin.

He came and stood next to her desk. Ruth looked up from papers she was only half reading.

"I leave tomorrow," said Jonah.

"I heard," said Ruth.

"I wanted to thank you for everything you've done for me," said Jonah.

"You were a gift to me," answered Ruth softly. "I have something for you."

She handed him a book with a thick leather cover and no title. Jonah took the book in his hands and thumbed its pages.

"The pages are blank," said Jonah.

"The pages in this book only appear blank," said Ruth. "This is your biography."

"I hope it will be a good book," said Jonah.

"Oh, it will," said Ruth, smiling, "I have already read some of the pages, and you begin wonderfully!"

Jonah grew boyfully shy with the compliment, and then hesitated, almost stumbled. "There is one more thing," said Jonah finally. "Please take care of Jacob. I know he cares very much for you."

"Yes," said Ruth, her eyes reassuring, "there is a wisdom of the heart in your pages."

And Now Let Us Say
Amen

Jacob helped Jonah put some of his clothes together in the same cloth bag Jacob had taken on his own journey many years earlier. When they finished, Jonah made tea. Then the two of them sat down together.

Jonah looked around him. "I will miss this room."

"This room will miss you," said Jacob, looking at the walls.

"Will you come to visit me, Jacob?" asked Jonah.

"I will already be there," said Jacob. "From the time I was a boy, whenever I saw the wind in the trees, I thought I was watching God breathing. Now, when you stand and feel the wind on your face or see it in the trees, I will be beside you."

Jacob continued: "There is a legend passed between the generations that explains why Noah chose to send forth a dove from the ark in search of dry land. It seems that all other birds when they grow tired find rest upon a rock or the limb of a tree. But when the dove grows tired, it does not cease flying. Instead, it rests one wing and flies with the other.

"On your journey," said Jacob, "may you have the strength to afford yourself rest. And in your absence, may I once again learn to fly with one wing."

Jacob rose from the table and placed the flat of his hands on Jonah's head. "May the Lord watch over and bless you," said Jacob. "May He cause His countenance to shine upon you and grant you peace. You have my blessing and love." Jacob hesitated for a moment and then added, "My son."

"Thank you," said Jonah. "What could be left to say?"

"And now let us say amen," said Jacob.

What Grows
Never Grows Old

Jonah set his bag down on the path. He turned and looked back toward the village. He could see the outline of Jacob and Ruth standing next to each other across the fields. The morning sky that had begun gray was shifting to blue.

He raised his hand and waved. Jacob returned the gesture. Jonah thought of shouting to Jacob, but a sudden gust of breeze tugged at his collar.

"I feel older watching him leave," said Ruth, resting her arm in the crook of Jacob's.

"What grows," said Jacob, "never grows old."

"Including love," added Ruth. And Jacob felt the warmth of her arm circling his.

Jonah turned one last time and, with the morning sun behind him, again raised his arm, waving to them across the distance.

THANK YOU

Andrew T. Krauss
Danyel benShea

"Only the hand that erases, creates."

© Marlan Globerson

ABOUT THE AUTHOR

NOAH BENSHEA is a poet, philosopher, and scholar. His books on *Jacob the Baker* are translated around the world and are embraced as timeless fables. Noah benShea's syndicated weekly column, "Noah's Window™," and its insightful message are read by countless readers. In addition, Mr. benShea is an adviser to North American community and business leaders. Born in Toronto, Noah benShea lives with his wife and family in Santa Barbara, California, where he is working on another book.